The Miracle Of Twin Rainbow Ridge

GEORGE SORBANE

ISBN:1976083540
ISBN-13: 9781976083549

TABLE OF CONTENTS

Chapter 1

In the Mountains Shadows

Deep within Central Appalachia country lays a small spot of houses that the local people called "Cold Hollow", spread along the foothills and hugging the lazy flow of Cacapon River. After the Great Depression hundreds of folks who have lost their small farms, jobs or any hope for subsistence up North, moved back to the safety of the mountains and away from ruthless bank collectors and enforcers, set-up a tent camp along the homestead of a local farmer named Archie Westwood, a homestead dating back all the way to the Civil War. When he finally heard that bunch of homeless people had invaded his property, he showed up on a gloomy, rainy day with his four sons, guns in hand, ready to expel the boarders.

But when Archie saw mothers with small children and old folks shivering under the cold rain in shanty, makeshift tents, he felt pity for the strangers, and instead gave them a large tent, two bushels of potatoes and few bundles of fire wood to help them fight the cold air sliding down from the mountains. Some folks stayed in the camp all the way to the war years of 1940, when Archie cut all of families a 50x50 feet parcel of land for five dollars each, setting up roots of the hamlet now known as the "Cold Hollow".

One of the men whose family took roots in Cold Hollow was a man named Glenmore Frances Tom, who had joined the Army in 1932 and rose to a rank of a Master Sergeant, just to be posted in Pearl Harbor a month before December 7, 1941.

When the Japanese sneak attack brought death and destruction to the island and the troops stationed there, he was one of the 2500 souls to tragically lose his life in an infamous war destined live forever in the annals of world history.

Glenmore's widow Tailor was left with her two sons and grandson Jimmy in the small three rooms house up on the hill until each one took his way and left her to raise the boy on her own.

So, Jim "Catfish" Tom grew with his grandma Taylor and her two dogs "Pony" and "Mush", two dogs that would often joined him on a hunt in the mountains or walk down the riverbanks on a sunny morning. Jim was ten years old when on one of these solitary walks in the woods he stumbled on a junk covered, overgrown weed grounds surrounding a shanty yellow school bus, with a blond-haired girl in small rubber boots and sporting faded jeans sitting on the wooden doorsteps, staring at him with her bright, blue eyes.

"Good morning to you, young Miss," Jim greeted her respectfully.

"I ain't no "Miss" to you and is nine years old. You can call me "Molly White Crain", the "Snake Girl". And who you might be stranger?"

"The call me Jim "Catfish" Tom, but you can call me "Jimmy"," he said.

"That's funny name," she smiled.

"Are they call you "Catfish" 'cos you look like one them or you catch lots of fish down the river?"

"I catch lots of cat fish by hand down in "Connell's sleeve corner,"" Jimmy admitted.

"I why you is the "Snake Girl"", Miss Molly?"

" 'Cos I've got a "Snake Power"" she said.

"Let me show you right now. You like snakes, Jimmy?" Molly started spreading her little hands in and out, like swimming in a water stream.

He could not believe his eyes when suddenly a

bunch of critters slid out the grass and right in front of her, clustering in a large circle, their heads up and all looking at her spreading low hisses.

"Now I want you to sleep and be peaceful," she said and moved her open hands down as to make them level with the ground.

They did coil flat, all silent in a nearly perfect circle to Jimmy's horror and amazement.

"You an amazing and beautiful girl, Miss Molly'" Jimmy praised her fearfully.

"And why you'd be of a "White Crain" name?"

"My mama is full blooded Indian of the Lakota tribe people. Hey mama, come 'on and meet my new friend Jimmy "Catfish" Tom," she hollered at the buss.

White hair woman with busted front tooth showed her face by the door, flashed a smile and got back inside. Jimmy noticed right away that Molly's eyes did not follow him, like he was a shadow, her blue eyes still staring at him without a wink.

"You is blind, ain't you miss Molly?" he carefully proposed.

"Kind of," she smiled.

"I see you as white shadow with curly hair, but can't see your face clearly. Mama sais I need a surgery, but we are so damn poor that can't even rent a decent house and get out of this school bus," she said sadly.

"If you is a rich man one day Jimmy, would please marry me and get me a surgery so I can see the world?" Molly pleaded shyly.

"I sure would, if I get lucky and you get rid of them crawling things," Jimmy promised.

"Ain't you fearing them critters, miss Molly? "

"I see them like red wiggles," she smiled.

"They ain't bad at all if you is to learn their speak," she said.

"I sure can show you if you would care to learn," she proposed.

"No thanks, Miss Molly!" Jimmy said smilingly.

"I reckon I would stick with the catfish for now," he said before heading back up the hill towards grandma's house.

And that is how all began, a chance meet that

later grew into a puppy love and more in later years, when Jimmy would walk Molly up the hill and carry her book to school, and even spend time to teach her how to handle numbers and read her stories. The number games soon changed him to the student, since she could multiply numbers in a flash while he can hardly do it in minutes.

"You are smarter than a pig with seeing eyes, let's forget a blind girl," he would joke at her.

"That is 'cos pigs are smarter than catfish, and better looking also," she would fight back at him.

"Have you ever been kissed by a pig Jimmy?" she would taunt him again.

"No, I wouldn't even if the pig were honey roasted, "he would laugh back.

"We'll see about that one of those days," she admonished him, running here long white fingers along his face, like trying to sense every tiny detail of his face, a detail she could only feel but not see.

"You are cow lick," she snapped in laughter.

"A catfish with a cow lick face, what in the world is that," Jimmy was clearly confused.

"The hair over your forehead is up like a cow licked your face, dummy," she mocked him again.

"I'll call a cow lick from now on, do you mind Jimmy?"

These games continued for quite a long time and one spring day Molly, then just about 14 years old said something that shattered the childish innocence that had kept a gulf of forbidden water between them.

"Do you like to kiss me Jimmy?" she whispered.

"A cow lick kissing a pig, that will be the day," he whispered back jokingly.

"I am not kidding, would you please try to kiss me, would you please Jimmy," she begged again.

Then their lips and hands met and Jimmy felt a river of passion run through his body, a shiver so primitive that he wanted to hold her tight close to him, but she pulled away with her hand pushing back on him, tears running down her face, whispering," Let's stop now, take me home, would you please Jimmy? My mom will surely kill me I she hears what happened today."

They came to be one day when her mom was

driven to the hospital for a surgery, and then sixteen-year-old Jimmy took Molly fishing down the river, spread a small tent he took from his uncle George in a small clearing in the forest. They roasted the steaks of the catfish on rocks buried in the fire, then went out for a swim on the banks, walked naked under the blue moon as two children that had sneaked out of god's den, joining into a passionate one many times next to crackling fire as raged clouds flew above uncovering clusters of bright starry skies above.

"I love you Jimmy," she said holding his hands, tears falling from her blue eyes.

"I know my mama will kill me if she found out what's happening, so we better go up the hill back and bring a lot's fish to put on her table."

Chapter 2

Drunken no good Molly Crains

Jim joined the Army in the spring of 1950 and soon found himself in a cold, rainy and hostile place called Pusan, squeezed by the advancing North Korean troops in a muddy valley, cornered between lake Chosin and a ring of hills above where the ticking sound of machine gun nest were sending fire to anything moving down below. A Turkish unit was stationed to the right, and soon Jimmy found a new friend, Sgt. Selim Chomukoglu, who had on many occasions led incursions behind enemy lines, sometimes bringing back a severed head of a Korean soldier who had been unfortunate to get across the grandsons of the soldiers of the Great Ottoman Empire, a message his superiors wanted to make blatantly clear to the North Koreans. Jim had been previously posted to the division heavy equipment maintenance arm, but the brazen North Korean attack had forced him to throw the wrenches and grab his rifle and join his unit and the Turks to defend a perimeter pinned down in the mud by relentless cold rain, howling winds and ever ticking sub machine gun on the hill above.

"I am sick and tired of them "Commies" terror shit, I am sick and tired of it," he complained to his friend Sgt. Selim Chomukoglu.

"I wonder I you would be willing to back me up in little terror of our own, to silence these bastards above and stop the daily death and carnage they are spilling on the soldiers in the muddy trenches below".

So he laid out his simple plan to Sgt. Chomukoglu: Every evening the machine nest above would stop ticking about 10 PM, when impenetrable darkness of low, gray clouds sending sheets of cold rain will cover the valley below. The Turkish unit would open fire at about 10:30 PM from left of the front, followed by some mortar and few heavy artillery fires. Meanwhile Jimmy, strapped with six hand grenades on his chest and armed with a small five rounds revolver would crawl up the hill and toss the grenades, two at a time to the two machine gun nests above, until they shut up or he is dead for sure.

"Beautiful plan, ain't it, Selim Aga?" he joked at the deeply concerned Sgt. Chomukoglu, whose eyes were carefully exploring the map of all positions along the front.

"Beautiful way to die my friend Jimmy, but

would my superiors endorse a suicide mission by an American, without orders from your own people? You better let your CO know about this before we both are court marshaled instead of being shot by the North Koreans."

Jimmy's CO, Lt. Raines Stoddard was enthusiastic about the plan from the onset.

"Jimmy, you shut up that nest above, I will make sure you get Purple Heart with onion and peeled potato cluster, I will peel the onions myself, you hear?" he joked.

"Just make you sure you don't get yourself killed by them Korean Commie's, they've been trained in karate and more deadly than wipers,"

"We will be waiting at the base of the hill, in case of firefight to get you down to safety."

As if by premonition, rain started soaking the valley with seething rage, and when Turks opened up on the right of the front, Jimmy crawled up the hill, six grenades strapped to his chest, small revolver in a hoister on left, eyes glued on the flashes from the North Korean machine gun nest above.

The barrage from below suddenly rose to

maddening hell, showering the troops above with fire and steel, Jimmy crawling up on his back, one with the mud, trying to gage the distance from the already burning trenches up on the hill.

At about fifteen feet, he tossed three grenades each at a teen feet dispersion at the position, followed by loud explosion and bright yellow flash that sent shower of mud and shrapnel over, just to see an outline of a North Korean soldier flying above, dagger in hand.

Jimmy fired one shot, then rolled down the hill, feeling lightning burning pain on the side of his skull and fingers, blacking out for minute or so.

When his mind and eyes came back to him, he was lying next to the dead North Korean soldier, a single shot blown a hole just above his eyes, the hill illuminated by the burning yellow flames of machine gun nest above.

He kept rolling down the muddy hill, the dead plants branches and small rocks sending streaks of red flashes of pain all over his body, until he blacked out again.

When Jimmy woke up, he was lying naked on a gurney, two medics cleaning him up, head and right arm bandaged, his friend Sgt. Selim and Lt. Stoddard right next to him.

"You one hard to kill SOB ain't you Jimmy? You got thirty-five shrapnel hits, bayonet gash on the side of the head, three right hand fingers tips shaved almost to the bone, and your heart still ticking as a brand-new cuckoo clock. I am telling you Sgt. Selim, those West Virginians are one hell of fighters, aren't they? And listen to this Jimmy, we took the hill and chase them Commie's all the way to the other valley. You rest now and we'll be back tomorrow, you hear?"

A morphine injection sent Jim into a heavenly world of crystal clear cool air under brilliantly white cloud cover with occasional rays of a bashful sun flashing like magic lighthouse deep in the sky.

He felt that his body is moving up and down in space, the bumps of the rough road sending arrows of flashing pain all over, then the sound of airplane propellers and sudden acceleration of takeoff giving his stomach sick feeling, his mind slowly slipping back into heaven.

When he opened his eyes again, Jimmy found himself in a Hospital room, his body bandaged all over, young nurse seating next to him, her green eyes attentively observing all his life signs and connections to the emergency monitors.

"You are safe now and everything will be alright. Doctor Wilson, Sgt. James Tom Francis is awake and ready for you if you would Sir," she hollered to the emergency desk.

Navy Commander in medical insignia with graying hair and big spectacle glasses entered, quickly going over Jimmy's life signs, then flashing a big, friendly smile at him.

"Our most distinguished patient seems to be improving quickly Nurse Redford, we just have to wait until bandages are all out to make sure there is no further infections going on."

"You know Sgt. Tom, the thirty-five shrapnel hits you got created a real danger for your health due to serious infections spreading in your blood stream. But they are all gone know, and I must say that all our team is honored to care for a true American hero like you, and won't be surprised if the Army finds a way to show Nation's deep appreciation of your selfless service."

Jim was deeply confused by the words, his mind still searching the hills of Pusan and ears hearing the ticking of the North Korean submachine nest up on the hill.

"Forgive me Dr. Wilson, where am I and why are me calling me Sergeant James Tom? Where is my unit and my friend Sgt. Selim? What happened to me?" his lips were cracked and throat dry, voice hardly audible, almost as a whisper.

"Sgt. James Tom, you were flown to the hospital ship Consolation due to severe injuries incurred in the explosion of the North Korean post in the valley of Koori, and promoted to a rank of sergeant on order by your division commander for extreme bravery and gallantry in the course of duty. Your unit and I am sure your friend Sgt. Selim is back on the offensive in Korea, but for you the war is over and shortly you will be on the way back to the States for a long recovery and therapy treatment. Now you take it easy, try to eat well and rest, and if you feel any discomfort at all at any time, alert the staff and they will be delighted and honored to take care of you, and this a direct order of Gen. MacArthur," Dr. Wilson gently shook Jimmy's left hand before leaving.

"Yes Sir," Jimmy obediently whispered, alone again, trying to adjust his body in a position that would minimize the pain, then falling in a deep, sweaty sleep, red lights and yellow tracers flying as if following him, then miraculously curving away and fading the distance.

The passage of time slowed to a crawl for Jimmy, many days passing until he was able to stand up on his own feet, sometimes staring through the oval cabin window at the harbor and coastline mired in fog and low clouds, trying to imagine how a war that was so brutal and unforgiving in one moment can all but disappear somewhere in the distance as if someone flipped a giant page in the book of his life and sending it in a new direction, engulfed in silence and loneliness.

Then the blessed day came when he was allowed to walk alone on the upper deck and mingle with other patient soldiers, listen to other heroes and share his own humble story. Walking in a sudden gust of cold wind or a shower of rain drops would flash a memory of the burning machine gun nest back in Pusan, then a vision of Molly would come back to him, so close and so real that he could smell the scent of flowers she used to pick at the banks of Cacapon river.

"It must be already snowing back home, I wonder if she misses me," Jimmy was talking to himself.

"I could write her a letter, but she won't be able to read it anyway, so I must be patient and fight that long wait until find myself back in the cold mountains and her warm embrace."

The soft vibration of the engines and a sudden blast of the ship's horn awakened Jim one Sunday morning, just to run outside and see a swath of waves splashing along with a white wake leaving the harbor and Korea in the distance.

"Ready to go home Jim?" Crewmember Gaynor Sims smiled at him.

"Hallelujah to that, brother can't wait to see my grandma's house huddled at the hills of Appalachia," joy rang in the voice of Jimmy, first time since the shootout with the Koreans when he felt his body bursting in strength, heart beating confidently, fists ready to take punch at life again.

"Where from in Appalachia?" Gaynor was curious.

"Cold Hollow, near Cacapon river junction."

"Well now, we almost like neighbors ain't we Jimmy? I come from Wooster, Ohio just up the road from your place. In about a week we should be in San

Diego, don't you worry".

"You think this tin can will make that far?" a whiff of fear crept in Jimmy's voice.

"Tin can, are you kidding me Jim, ours is an excellent ship, just make sure the captain does not hear you griping, 'cos he may get mad and toss you over the side and keep your Purple Heart as a souvenir," Gaynor threatened jokingly.

Jimmy was flabbergasted by the joke.

"Ain't got no Silver Star or any Heart at all," he countered in fear and disappointment.

"Where did you hear that gossip?"

"A friend of mine told me that you are due a Purple Heart for bravery, an Ataturk medal from your Turkish friends and a South Korean campaign medal for gallantry in battle. Just be patient Jimmy, it takes quite a while until the brass get the things rolling. All of us on this ship are very proud to have you aboard, you brave West Virginian"; Gaynor warmly shook Jimmy's hand, and then saluted him on the way to his station.

No one ever gave a praise or decoration to

Jimmy all his life, and all of sudden he felt like being on an enormous stage under a river of flashes from the news cameras, in front of thousands of people saluting him and his bravery in the duty to his country, bravery that in his humble heart he had already forgotten.

"At least someone remembered me," tears flowed down his cheeks, a lump in the throat took his breath faraway for a moment, his trembling fingers pulling Molly's picture from his pocket trying to see her face through his clouded, moist eyes.

"Would be proud of me also Molly baby, would you? If you do, I'll be the happiest man in Cold Hollow, I really would," Jim kept talking to himself, then a cloud of suspicion came over him.

"Talking to one self is just crazy, cat crazy," his practical mind reckoned, his eyes dried from the tears and heart coming to a peaceful beat.

"Let's wait and see the blue shores California and feel the warmth of being home again back in Appalachia, then Molly Crains will be the one the to greet me with a loving embrace or lead me away from the doors of loneliness," Jim's faced the cold wind, staring at the white weak of the ship fading in the distance.

"I must be strong and relentless like the ever-raging waves, soar like a seagull in the endless blue sky, and then and only then the Manitou of the ocean will fill my soul with an everlasting sense of being part of the forever being called God," his hands were clinching the white ship's railing with strength he never felt in his life, lungs full with air, blood pumping in his veins.

"Wait James Francis Tom, son of the mountains, wait until the next page of life is visible to you, be tall and proud as Mount Rushmore and patient as the drizzling rain of Appalachia," thoughts were rolling in his mind like waves approaching a welcome shore, ready to splash into spectacular cloud of water drops, just waiting to shine all colors of the rainbow.

Chapter 3

In Rich Man's Shoes

It took two weeks for the ship to moor in San Diego Harbor where he was transferred to the Naval Hospital for a month of recovery followed by final examination of his health, and then in a short and somber ceremony he was awarded his Purple Heart, Order of Ataturk and South Korean Campaign Medal, honorably discharged and on the way back home to Appalachia.

A freezing rain and mountains hiding snow covered peaks under a sky of scattered low, grey clouds welcomed Jim first steps back home, back home to grandma's embrace, tears in her eyes and voice chocking in sorrow of the early passing of his uncle George.

Jim never knew his father and George has been like a father to him all his life, so he walked up the hill to the snow-covered cemetery and then stayed silent under the falling rain for a long, long time, staring at the simple wooden cross and frozen flowers friends had left at his side, unable to comprehend why the cruel fate has taken the only man who would have understood the depths of his victory over clash with death, himself being a distinguished Veteran of a Great War.

When darkness was about to fall over the mountains, Jim finally broke his bond with the sorrow and found strength to walk down the river to Moly Crain's place, just to get another cold gust of winter in his heart.

The tears of Molly were warm and relentless, her hands and trembling fingers searching the downs of his face, voice whisper soft, but words soon turning desperate and stone cold sending chills to his heart.

"I was afraid they would kill you out there and was praying for you every day love, praying that you don't come home in a body bag. I love you James Francis Tom, I always will and would like to marry you now or forever, but I don't want to bring a child to this world that would live in a yellow school bus down the river in a relentless misery, just to face slow death from black lung like my father Gordon or get crushed fixing a junk car like my brother Mike."

"Hell, we are so poor that I cannot even see the man I am supposed to marry, because we don't have few thousands of dollars to pay for my surgery and be blessed to see the world, the endless joy to be with my husband and my children. Save me dear Jim, save us and our love," she begged, kissing his eyes and lips, her blind eyes searching the space around him.

"You smell like a moonshine pit, have you been drinking Mollie Crains?" he could not help but taste the booze in her kiss.

"Cousin Christie gave me a jar of shine and took a lick or two," she smiled dimly.

"Now a lick or two, tomorrow a gulp or two and there goes a bucket of hillbilly moonshine and trip to jail or worse," he snapped at her.

"Promise me no more booze if you love me, would you Molly Crains?"

"I would if I can help it?" she said holding his both hands as he left the yellow school bus.

Walking up the hill in the falling darkness and whirls of frozen show, his mind was going over of everything Molly had just said, the whip of the words still slapping his ears, his mind trying to get around the desperate wall of ice that had just fallen between him and Molly.

"It simple, so simple that I wonder how I never thought of it, I must be rich, very rich," a flash of hope came to him as he came to grandma front door.

"Nana, I must be rich and Molly would marry me," he charged in and grabbed her hands, just to notice the strange look in her eyes.

"You are rich Jimmy, Uncle George left you his house up the hill and all his possessions within. I never told you that but George was actually your father, and he helped raise you after your mother's untimely death. Don't you worry son, everything will turn alright, I know it will."

Two days later Jim found a job in the garage of Mr. Henry Corroders, a job of heavy duty mechanic handling the vehicles of West Virginia Transportation District paying the incredible sum of $62.92 per week, his first step to his goal of being a rich man.

But the fate still had few trump cards for him hidden in its sleeves, after hardly a week had passed on his new job when Mr. Corroders surprised him with unusual inquiry that would have never crossed his mind at all.

"Hey Catfish, you in trouble with the law or something?"

"No Mister Sheriff, I ain't coming back to jail," the silver voice of Jimmy sang from the pit down below.

"You say not, but then why is this lawyer man named Mr. Emmett Dwight Barnes looking for you, and even leaving his card and a phone number for you to call collect?" Mr. Corroders could hardly keep his confusion.

The bright, beaming face of Jimmy adorned by two brilliant brown eyes popped out right from below the truck.

"You says what, a lawyer looking for me, I ain't done nothing wrong so far, hardly been back home for two weeks? Let me see that business card would you Mr. Corroders? I will try to call him during my lunch break," he could hardly hold his breath, his heart unable to wait and see what hand of cards the Providence may deal to him.

The call to Attorney Barnes brought even more incredible news.

"Your Uncle George left his estate to you, including a bank account worth 25,000 dollars, 4000 acres of mountain land adjacent to his anthracite coal mine claim in the "Twin Rainbow Ridge District" and nearly 5000 tons of mined coal, ready for delivery at current price of $35 per ton. Meet me at 8 AM tomorrow at Lorry's diner if you can, so we can sign all-important papers and start things rolling for you. Please bring forms two picture ID's like a driver's license and maybe a military discharge certificate," Attorney Barnes said in conclusion.

Mr. Corroders was happy to see Jimmy move to possibly better things in life, but added:

"Let's hope your trek as a rich man brings all happiness the world dishes at you, yet I hate to lose such fine man and worker like you. Feel welcome to come back anytime if things don't pan out as expected."

Next morning Jimmy was in Lorry's diner sharp at 8 AM, having hardly slept through the night, his mind rolling endlessly in a maze of questions he wanted to ask about his newly found future, eyes peeking through window, scanning the grey sky above and the lonely road for the magic Attorney Barnes, the man who had all of a sudden created an infinite enigma in his life.

A green station wagon Jeep finally pulled over outside, and bespectacled grey haired gentleman, clearly Attorney Barnes walked in and straight to his table.

"Good morning, I am very pleased to meet you Jimmy, you are James Frances Tom ain't you?" he smiled and warmly shook his hand.

"Before we start discussing the paperwork, I need to see the two forms of personal picture ID I requested previously, do you mind Jimmy?"

"You are decorated war hero, I hear? Your uncle George was incredible proud of your service, as are all of us that had the privilege of meeting you, I am sure?"

Jimmy was starting to like Attorney Barnes, like the warm and down to earth old fashion sincerity and trust he seem to exude.

"Here is the folder with the final will papers, and I would like you to sign on the dotted line down here, indicating that I have disclosed to you the basic parts of holdings of Uncle George. By the way, I failed to mention that the proven coal reserves of the mine in the Twin Rainbow Ridge are estimated to be worth some 25 million dollars at current prices, and the value of the land is another 10 million according to an estimate you will find within the final papers, which makes the value of your estate to some 36 million dollars. In addition, your uncle purchased a month ago three room fully furnished rental property with gas heat, about a mile up the road from here, and you will also find the keys and papers in the folder I gave you. Do you have any questions Jimmy, please don't hesitate to ask at any time if the burden of being a young millionaire starts to play on your nerves and makes you uncomfortable?"

"Here it comes another pleasant surprise," Mr. Barnes smiled, pointing to a red Studebaker convertible that just had pulled next to his Jeep.

A young man in his twenties entered the diner and stopped by their table, handling him a set of car keys.

"Jimmy, I would like you meet by son Mitch who drove in the car your dear Uncle George bought for you three weeks before your return from Korea, she is pretty one ain't she?"

All this heaps of love were getting too much for Jimmy, like someone who had loved and cared for him so much had laid a red carpet for him, red carpet leading to answer all his fears and obstacles the words of Molly Crains had greeting him with. Tears started running down on his cheeks, tears of joy that the fate had granted him all his dreams, and denied him the chance to meet and give a warm hug to dear Uncle George one more time before his untimely passing, instead of fighting a deadly war with the North Koreans.

"War heroes are not supposed to cry, but I cannot help it, so please try to understand," he mumbled, choked by tears and trying to breathe through heavy lump in his throat.

"Before we close shop for today gentlemen, I wonder if you Attorney Barnes may be able to help me with a medical question I have regarding my girlfriend Mollie Crains. She suffers from an early childhood partial blindness condition that some doctors have diagnosed as curable, and I wonder if you can recommend a surgeon that can correct her vision by all means necessary, since money is not an issue at this point in time."

"I would be delighted to help, and in few days, you will get a call indicating whom and where you must meet and time of the appointment if any. Again, it has been a pleasure to meet you, Jimmy, and I and my office are at your disposal at any time," Attorney Barnes and Mitch shook his hand before leaving.

Jimmy finally realized that he was in trouble now, having have to drive old Ford truck and the shiny spanking new red Studebaker back to Uncle George house, a time of decisions that was to crown his new life as an owner of property and money.

But first, he decided to walk outside and take a look at the cutie nestled next to his window. Having driven junk cars all his life, his breath took a dive when he opened the door of the red Studebaker, just to be met by the meticulous white leather interior and working radio, then by a V8 engine huddled under the hood.

"This lady is prettier than Molly Crains," the joke was already running around his mind.

"I should just drive down the river to Molly's yellow bus, then give her the surprise news of her life," he planned his next move when fireman Charlie Croons stopped by.

"Hey Catfish, you did not snatch this pretty baby, did you?" he sounded in disbelief.

"No Croony I didn't, but you can make five bucks if you drive my truck back to Uncle George's house, then I'll drive you back so you can buy yourself a steak dinner, you interested buddy?"

"Hell, I am so hungry that for five bucks I'll follow you to earths end, bud," Charlie could not hide his amazement that fate had smiled at him on a such cold afternoon.

Soon the old Ford truck was on Uncles George's driveway, Charlie back in the diner and Jimmy driving the shiny Studebaker from the end his seat down the road to Molly's place, his heart pounding when even a rain drop would drop on the hood.

Knock on bus door and her she was, holding his hand on the way to the red Studebaker.

"Did you paint your truck red," she hollered, able to see the color but not the shape of the car itself.

"No I did not, but the good Lord whisper in the ear of my dear Uncle George to will me his estate, and now I am millionaire and you will have your surgery within few months. Let's set the old yellow buss afire, then go the preacher and say I do," Jimmy proposed victoriously.

"Set the yellow bus afire with my whole family in it, and all little critters all over the bushes, are you crazy or something Catfish," she hollered at him.

"Well then, get all of you dressed up I will be back in about half an hour to show the new house you are moving in, and then we all are going out for a steak dinner down in the "Wolf Claw" lounge", Jimmy slapped a kiss on her lips and ran back to car.

Driving slowly up the road in the drizzling rain, his heart missing a beat anytime a swat of raindrops pounded his beautiful new car, about two miles up the roads Jimmy soon spotted a one-story house snugged between overgrown trees lot, house number "Acme Street 115" plainly visible on the mailbox.

He walked along the gravel-covered driveway to the front door that opened with a grudging squeak, greeted by the warm smell of the pine veneer covered living room.

"Uncle George has left a lot of good will and love in this house," he thought aloud, wiping the tears streaming down his cheeks, walking like in a trance around the house appointed with homely early American furniture.

"Holly cow, this thing has a gas heat and even a refrigerator. I better fully stock it up with goodies before the family comes in. If Molly Crains had the eyes to see this, she would have cried million tears of happiness. Thank you, Uncle, may you rest in peace on the right side of the Lord," he mumbled, all chocked up by goodness that had fallen upon him.

A quick stop to the general store to fill Studebaker's trunk with groceries, then back on the road again, stocking-up Mollie's fridge to the hilt and dropping the rest to Grandma Taylor kept his mind busy, trying to calm down and let his tears subside before facing Molly's family.

They were all waiting already, and he let Molly and her Mom sit next to him, then helped Gordon and Mike be comfortable in the back seat, both clearly confused by such a stunning turn of events, yet beaming of excitement and amazement being in such a beautiful red car.

But this was just the beginning. When the front door was opened and the family walked in the cozily appointed new house, sounds of wailing and tears burst from Molly and her Mom, unable to understand that all this is for them.

"Yes, it is all for you, just relax and enjoy it," Jimmy assured them, trying to keep his own emotions in check and pretend to be confident and assertive.

"I cannot see it all, but the sweet smell of pine

and feeling of this house is so beautiful, we can never find enough thanks to say to you," Molly tightly held his hands, giving him a hug and warm kiss, her chest trembling from the tears.

"All right you all all right, enough tears for one day, just give me second to make a small announcement," Jimmy tried to stop and downwards spiral of emotions that had overcome every one.

"And now ladies and gentleman, may I have the envelope please?" Jimmy finally found the strength to make a joke and get the mood of everybody up and shining.

"It is my pleasure to introduce you all to the best part of the evening. We are picking up Grandma Taylor and then driving some twenty miles down the road to the "Wolfs Paw" for a steak dinner. Or perhaps someone may prefer catfish? We can go down to the Connell's cove, break the ice and try to catch some," he quipped as everybody streamed out.

"Oh shut up with the catfish Jimmy, and let's pick up Grandma right now and get going," Molly held his hand, her eyes adoringly scanning his face, as if desperately trying to see through the curtain of blindness the man she loved so much.

Soon Grandma Taylor was sharing the front seat, and Molly in the back with Gordon and Mike, the Studebaker gallantly gliding the lonely road, road embraced by cold and snow covered mountains like leading to nowhere, but that was only an illusion.

The "Wolf Paw" was nestled among the hills and greeted them with soft lights, kind and smiling people and warm, early American setting, amplified by pictures of Appalachian pioneers, old rifles and mining gear that would have made anyone feeling at home. The magic lights of the jukebox and few nickels brought music that made eyes moist with tears, and there they were, a loving circle of people that by the miracle good will of Uncle George had transgressed the boundaries of a society that understood only the language of money, money and only money.

Molly had a request.

"I would love to hear Patty Page's song "Tennessee Waltz,"" she whispered in Jimmy's ear.

"Would you play it for me darling, I have heard it so many times on my radio," she softly caressed his check with her hand.

"I will play it if you dance with me," he demanded jokingly, dropping another nickel in the Jud box.

"If I were blessed with eyes to see this world clearly, I would love to see Tennessee and Cape Cod one day," Molly continued whispering in his ear.

"See Tennessee and Cape Cod alone, with some else or with me, or I'll want my nickel back," Jimmy demanded threateningly.

"With you dummy, don't you know that I'll love you forever," she again caressed his ear with her fingers.

"I've asked Att. Barnes to arrange for an appointment with an eye doctor to see if a surgery can rectify your ailment, and if possible to suggest a hospital where the treatment can be done. So, Cape Cod may not be so far away baby," Jimmy smiled, having finally revealed the secret held just for this moment.

"Mom, did you hear that, I am to have surgery and able to see, "Molly embraced her mother, both sobbing in tears.

"Hold on now, hold on, please let not get too excited and wait to hear from the doctor," Jimmy cautioned softly, realizing that his big news may turn into a tragic abyss should the answer to cure turns out to be negative.

"Let's eat now and forget about tomorrow," he tried to turn the attention to the happy and loving evening, away from the potholes of the world.

"It was always my dream to go back to old Mother England and visit my folk's town of Chester, North-West of London," Gordon admitted, dimly staring at the snow-covered hills outside.

"My great-grandpa came to the Americas in 1829, lived in Boston for a while then settled down in Ohio," he continued his story

"We may arrange a visit one day pops, but first I am about to get you an oxygen bottle service to help you breathe easily, and have Mike seen by a doctor to get some therapy with his legs. Let's take care of the steaks, before wolfs snatch them away," Jimmy joked again.

"And if I may propose toast, let's lift our wine glasses and remember dear Uncle George, may he rest in peace," his voice broke from emotion, eyes full with tears.

"To George, may he live forever," glasses rang

in remembrance.

"I now propose another toast to Grandma Taylor, we all love her, don't we," glasses rang again in admiration.

Molly was worried.

"Jimmy, you think you can drive back after all this wine, darling? You are our only driver, would please cut down on the shine, would you please?"

The warmth and charm of the evening seemed to last forever, as if their souls were huddled above them in a chain of love and remembrance that made the passage of time stop for a while, at least till one pass midnight, when the bartender whispered in Jim's ear that is time to go home.

All back in the red Studebaker, floating in the night covered road under rags of wet snow coming in never ending stream in the enormous windshield that made the eye feeling like the car was about to plow in the pines covered hill. By the time Jim was in front of Grandma's house everyone but Molly was deep asleep, then one by one he guided them to their front door.

When Jim was finally back home, he lit the fireplace, then laid on the couch covered with warm blanket and kept watching the dance of the flames as if trying to find the answer to why his destiny took on the road he never had dreamed of being onto.

The morning light sneaked through the ice crystal covered windowpanes, sending chills to his body and warm vapor clouds flying above his lips. He fired another batch of logs in the fireplace, then lit the gas stow and waited until the heat was high enough to fry some eggs and boil a cup of coffee.

For first time in his life, Jim Francis felt as a happy man, man in love with beautiful yet partially blind woman, a lot of money in the bank, brand new red Studebaker and a lot of people who adored and loved him. Yet in the back of his mind, there was a flurry of worries, a feeling of guilt that he never been to his Uncle's coal mine and other properties that were the backbone to his future.

"On the first break of the weather I must go up the mountain to Twin Rainbow Ridge and pay homage to my Uncle's legacy and his memory," he decided, going outside to take a look at the Appalachian sky, covered with low, gray clouds sending small, ice like flakes of snow. It took almost a week before a blue sky greeted him one cold March morning, when Jim took his rifle, Uncle's revolver, warm clothes, compass and plenty of food, giving Molly a warm kiss goodbye and then driving the green Jeep on the winding road up the mountain.

Driving on the frozen dirt roads was treacherous and deadly, the tires sliding on the ice-covered curves, the Jeep tilting against the grade, ready to roll down hill and throw Jim in a frozen wilderness that has been probably untouched since the Creator made Appalachia.

Yet Jim would not budge and back down, and so after about two hours of struggle with the mountain, his map led him to a flat curve, nestled under an ugly and hostile looking hill at the bottom of which there was a mining shaft and large blue sign, "Dig #17" with an abandoned white chapel on the left.

A small aged pine trailer office and a gated, barbed wire backyard where a large pile of shiny chunks of anthracite coal were lined up against the hill next to tarp-covered machinery.

"This must be my fortune," a joke flashed in Jim's mind as he turned the key in the rusted door lock, finding himself in a small office where stacks of receipts covered the old deck and wall photo of Uncle George holding a young child in his arms sending a flood of tears to his eyes.

"You were my daddy, weren't you Uncle George," his voice broke into dry, helpless cry, his heart finally realizing the truth behind the selfless, unconditional love he was blessed with since his earliest remembrance.

It was cold and stuffy in the office, so Jim lighted fire under few logs of lumber in the cast iron stove, then threw two large chunks of coal in and soon it was warm and cozy, so cozy that he sat down in the desk chair and went through all papers stuffed in the drawers, until a small family album caught his eye.

There was a faded picture of a beautiful young woman with a Marlene Dietrich hairdo and attire, labeled "Ingrid Bedenbacher", Newport News, 1936. Then there was another photo of Ingrid holding a two or three-year-old baby boy, next to a man looking like young Uncle George in an Army uniform, signed "June 3, 1939, San Francisco".

Jim felt like falling into a bottomless pit, his chest trembling from emotion, realizing that he may have inadvertently stumbled upon a tightly guarded family secret.

"I was always told that my father was Uncle

George's twin brother Melvin who went missing in the battle of Guadalcanal, and that my mother Carolyn, succumbed to ill health in Hawaii. I was then adopted by Uncle George and raised by Grandma Taylor. Who in the world is Ingrid Bedenbacher? I wonder what granny has to say about this," Jim extinguished the stow fire, locked up the office and then started walking to his Jeep. Something caught his eyes when he looked at the aged, crumbling chapel nestled under overgrown trees covering the hill; it was the front door that was flapping to the gust of the wind, emitting crying like noise, like asking him to come and help. He walked through the mud-covered lot, carefully climbing the wet, cracked steps and pushed the door open. A dingy smell of decaying wood and few rays of light coming from the broken windows sent shivers in his bones, a feeling of danger one can sense but cannot see.

"This place smells like an open grave," Jim thought, tying the door to the frame with a piece of rope, then slowly walking back to the Jeep.

"I better have someone cleanup this relic once I get the money," he though, his eyes searching the cloudy, freezing rain drenched sky on the way to the valley.

"I wonder if Consolidated Mines Terminal is still open," he wondered, made a left turn toward the train track and then to the coal covered lot of the scales bin. There was no one in sight, so he turned around and took the road back to Cold Hollow. Frozen rain was turning to snow already, sending the Jeep sliding to the curb and then back, until Jim came close to the dark and seemingly abandoned train station. A silhouette of a tall man covered with snow caught his eye, standing next to the track with a small black suitcase next to him.

Jim drove by and rolled down the window.

"What are you doing man, waiting for Santa Claus? You got a name reindeer?

" There ain't no Santa Claus for me Sir, and they calls me Marshal Beam," the man dusted the snow from his face, flashing a dim smile.

"You got a roof man?" Jim continued.

"No Sire, I just came from Alabama to look for a new start after spending six year in the slammer," Marshal divulged.

"Six year for what Marshal, what did you do?" Jim continue pressing.

"I slapped a police officer down in Montgomery for calling me a honey ass n... r," he smiled, wiping the melting snow from his face.

"That's funny, very funny Marshal but you should thank the good Lord they did not lynch you," Jim contended.

"Boy do I hate them white trash red necks down South, tough on poor people, shitting their pants in the war," he continued.

"Are you looking for job Beam? Are you really looking for a new start, or a lull before back to jail? My name is Jim Frances Tom and need a coal yard man, ten dollars per week plus housing and you can drive this Jeep. You think you might be interested?"

"I'll do anything to keep your trust in me Mr. Tom," Beam exclaimed.

"I left wife and four children down in Alabama, alone with no money or property to care for," his eyes were full with tears.

"Well then Mr. Beam, do we have a handshake?" Jim extended his hand to him.

"Yes Sire, we have a handshake, and I will not

disappoint, I promise," Marshal enormous hand grabbed Jim's.

"All right then, hop in and let me drive you to the Ashley's motel down in the valley," Jim said before taking down the road.

Warren Ashley wasn't happy seeing a black person coming to his motel.

"Are you crazy Catfish, dragging this n... r to my property? You want them red necks to burn me down by tomorrow morning?" his eyes were burning with fear, hand gesturing wildly.

Jim was not in the mood to listen to that crap.

"You listen to me Warren Ashley, and listen very good. This man's name is Marshal Beam and he's my yard man up the mine, so you better tell them mama lies hillbillies that if he loses a feather, I am going to hunt them down and burn their asses. I am giving you sixty dollars' advance for you to take care of him for a week, shotgun in hand, because if you don't I'll buy the lot across the road and dump so much coal on it, that when you look at your sorry face in the morning, it will look just like his cousin's ass," he threatened on the way out.

Marshal Beam was frightened by the words.

"Mr. Francis, I don't want to be trouble to you, let me stay in the train station, it will be safe for both of us," he begged.

"Don't you worry Marshal, I will pass the word to Sheriff Hatchet that you are staying in town, and everything will turn alright, just keep your head low, you hear?"

Once Jim had passed the word to Sheriff's office, there was nothing to do, but pick-up Molly and get a lunch in the diner.

But his mailbox had a surprise letter for him. Attorney Barnes had gotten in touch with a Cleveland eye surgeon named Jeffrey Manning, and scheduled an exploratory eye exam for Molly Crains on April 14, 1957, just thirty days away.

Things were lining up for James Frances Tom, finding a yardman for his coalmine and having a meeting with a doctor who may realize Molly Crains lifelong dream to see the world. He waited until they were seated in the corner of the room, then held her hands and whispered, "I have something to say to you if you promise me that you will not cry or scream, you promise?" his fingers caressed her blind eyes, lips kissing her forehead.

It seemed that Molly could not immediately absorb the dimension or the meaning of the good news, just mumbling, "I've been waiting for this for a lifetime dear."

"Please don't kindle too much hope in mom's and pap's hearts for a miracle, let's be patient and pray that our dream will come true. I have few more things to take of before we go," Jim promised before dropping her to the house.

Two days later a break in the weather gave him a chance to drive to the mine with Marshal Beam and give him a quick prep for the job he was to do while working alone and delivering coal to the Consolidated Mines Terminal down the valley.

The small bedroom and office was first cleaned up and new linens and pillows left on the bed, all windows were scrubbed from the coal dust and caulked, and finally the water pump and gasoline engine res-started and checked out.

Then Jim gave Marshal a lesson how to load coal on the sorter, remove residue and small rocks, then wash the lumps squeaking clean, ready for delivery to the terminal. A quick trip downhill led them to the office of one Sanford Gray, scales foreman who was surprised to see a black man working for Jim.

"You sure made our mind quickly choosing Marshal to be a yard man, didn't you Catfish?" he flashed a smile through his missing front teeth.

"Yes I did, and if someone has problem with that, they better talk to me and not him, do you read me Sanford? Spread the news around and let him be! I'll take care of any issues when back from Cleveland," Jim words were hard and nearly threatening.

"You sure I won't get lynched by them hillbillies Mr. Francis, I is afraid to work alone in the mountain?" the voice of Marshal Beam was trembling, his long fingers tapping on his knees in fear.

"I'll let Sheriff Hatchet know that you are alone doing my business for a few weeks, and ask him to pass by the mine from time to time to check you out. I am also giving you one hundred dollars to cover your salary for a month, the rest used to buy gas for the truck and other expenses.

"You should try to deliver at least three loads of coal per day, keep all receipts handy on the left side of the office table. Now drive down the mountain and drop me home," Jim ordered before Marshal took over the Jeep.

Sheriff Hatchet was not pleased to have a black man in his backyard running a coalmine.

"You one crazy son of a gun to leave a felon as a yard man, ain't you Catfish," he growled in disapproval.

"I'll do it, but if he starts trouble, you'll find him rotting in jail when you come back," he threatened.

"Let him be Sheriff, and if everything turns for the better, I'll do something for your officers; how about brand new booths, new radio and spanking cold 45 straight out of the box?" Jim promised before leaving.

Even though he had set the mine to operate without him, the thought of Ingrid Bedenbacker was still on his mind.

"I better send a letter with copy of her photo to my Army buddy Elmer Quinsy up in New York, his private detectives may dig out where she is, that is if she is still alive. Except Grandma Taylor, she'll be the last family I have left," thoughts of worry were flying through his mind.

The time was flying fast and finally on March 4, 1957, Jim, Molly and her Mom Sarah took the road North to Cleveland in the red Studebaker on wet roads hugging the mountain covered still with snow.

They made it to the Roadside Inn in Wooster, Ohio by the sundown, then by the early afternoon next day Cleveland greeted them with sparse sun and light clouds.

Attorney Barns had made a reservation in Motel 6 on Superior Avenue, just few streets from Dr. Manning's office.

They had a dinner across the streets in Manny's tavern, and then huddled in front of the fireplace with drink in hand, thinking of the momentous day that was awaiting them.

But as many times in life, the fear of the unknown may be greater than expectation of the known.

After an hour of intense examination, Dr. Manning appeared in the waiting room with a lot good, and some bad news.

"Molly is young, very strong, blood pressure below my expectation, and I think she has excellent chance of re-gaining her vision within a few days after surgery. The bad news is that she needs to be admitted in the Hospital for a week, and the expense of that and surgery may reach up to four thousand dollars. Are you in position to afford this amount?" his eyes intensely groped Jim's face.

"That will not be a problem," Jim assured him.

"You are welcome to talk to Attorney Barnes about funding that, or I can simply write a check for the amount," a mountain a fear and worry suddenly melted as if in a miracle from his chest, as Molly and her Mom embraced, tears falling from their eyes.

"Well then, Molly need to report to the surgery preparation room at 6 AM tomorrow morning, and will perform the surgery from 11 AM till about noon. Then barring next day post-surgery examination, she will start her recovery program," Dr. Manning shook Jim hand before leaving.

Next morning at 6 AM Mollie was all set and prepped by the staff for the pre-surgery test, then rolled in the surgery room.

For Jim, there was nothing else to do but walk

across the street, get a breakfast and scour the morning paper for the latest news. Hour or so later he walked back to the Hospital and took a seat in the waiting room, his mind starting to roll into circles of what and why may happen if things did no go as planned.

He must have snoozed up for a while when felt that someone gently touched his shoulder, whispering," Mr. Francis, the surgery is over and now you can come and see the patient."

He followed her confusingly, his heart beating loudly and throat dry from fear, just to enter the room and see Molly Crain's face blindfolded across the eyes and young nurse checking her vital signs.

"I am Dr. Heather Ringwald and I am in charge of post-surgery procedures and follow-through. Ms. Crains must avoid sunlight for at least a week, after which she will be required to wear special dark glasses for a month until Dr. Manning is completely satisfied by her recovery. You are allowed to visit every day from 10 AM to 2 PM until she is released from the Hospital," she smiled before leaving the room.

Overcome by fear and dark suspicion, Jim pulled a chair and sat right next to Molly's bed, just to feel that her fingers searched for his hand, and soft whisper asking," Will I be able to really see the world, or is this some kind of rude joke, will I, Jimmy Francis Tom?"

He kissed his hot and very dry lips, then found the strength to whisper back," The Doctor said that in a week you should be able to see the world though special dark glasses, just have a fate and everything will turn alright," his fingers caressed her lips while his heart pounding in fear of the unknown.

"Will I be able to see you for first time in real colors, see you really pretty," she again searched the Universe that was awaiting her.

"I hope you'll won't be disappointed when you see me, 'cos I fell in love with you the moment I laid eyes on you in the yellow school bus of yours," he tried to lighten up the air, still unsure what the future will bring to them next week.

Days in a world covered by dark shades of fear flew slow and painfully until a week after, when the day they have been waiting for all her life came to be: Molly's blindfold was taken out, and then she slowly opened her eyes into the dim light of the room after many excruciating moments of terror searching for him, then rushed and held him in her arms.

"I can see you sweet little man, I can see how pretty you are," she screamed in excitement, and then a cloud of suspicion came over her.

"Do I also look pretty like you, do I," tears fell off her eyes as Jimmy was leading towards the bedroom mirror.

"Is that me Jimmy, this woman with blue eyes and pale blond hair, do you think I am pretty for you?" she continued to scream as suppressed feelings were surfacing from her memory.

"I ain't never seen anybody prettier that you," he assured her joyfully, putting his lips to her cheek and slapping a kiss while holding her tenderly.

"Just wait and see until we arrive in Cape Cod and get married in the Hoxie House in Sandwich, Massachusetts. You'll be the prettiest bride on that shore since the Pilgrims landed there," Jimmy continued joking, holding her hands and trying to exude confidence and happiness in her new life.

It took nearly a week for all tests by the surgeons' office to declare Molly Crains surgery a complete success, and then Jimmy took back on road to the distant shores where the founders had landed nearly three hundred years ago, as Molly sporting her dark glasses and her Mom kept watching the unfolding and unfamiliar flat, green trees lined roads leading to Pennsylvania mountains.

After nearly five days of driving through the country, the red Studebaker finally started following narrow winding roads surrounded by patches of small sand dunes until finally at the distance there was blue shine of the ocean, bright, white small waves rushing to the shore.

The Hoxie house turned out to be an old, colonial two stories stone home dating all the way back to the Founders, and the house keeper kindly helped them to set in their rooms, adorned by old English like furniture and souvenirs from times passed by.

An enormous, wood-burning fireplace on the first floor was exuding warmth and sweet smell of pinesap, with a bottle of sherry awaiting them on the table adorned with plate of young turkey stuffed with apples, and 19th century plates and silver made utensils ready for their culinary pleasure.

Molly has never experienced such a luxury,

incessantly walking around, taking a look through the narrow, old fashioned windows outside, then would hold his hands and look at him with eyes full with tears.

"You sure this place is for us Catfish, I feel we don't belong in here", she could not help but open her fears about this new, beautiful but unknown new world.

"Yes I am sure and if ever there was anybody who belong here, it is us and especially you and Mom dearest," Jim smiled, then giving her a tender kiss on the lips.

"Just wait till tomorrow for our short but very charming wedding ceremony in old "Pilgrims Chapel", then I'll drive you guys to Cape Cod pier for a candlelight dinner on a table with an ocean view," he smiled again.

Winds picked up during the night and curtains of raindrops flapped on the windowpanes, as the century's old trees outside moaned and twisted to wild and scary gusts blowing from the ocean. Listening to sounds of pulsing and banging howls of the storm, one could not help but wonder if someone nearby was recounting for them the haunting story of the brave people who took that life and death journey to freedom through the violent and unpredictable waters of the North Atlantic nearly three hundred years ago.

The morning met them with sunny, blue skies as a knock on the door by the local tailor announced the arrival of Molly brand new, white wedding gown encrusted with hand sown white rosses on the sides. A short drive to Cape Cod Chapel unraveled yet another surprise: It was an old, white cut stones room with heavy wooden front door, and a simple wooden cross behind the pulpit.

Pastor Roy Jenkins and a choir of two women and a middle-aged man started singing after the short prayer that he uttered:" May the Lord All Mighty Bless All," and then something in the bright harmony of their voices struck a note of sadness in Jim's heart, a remembrance of dear Uncle George who's passing has been on his mind for a year, a whiff of sorrow that he couldn't be here now in this proud and elevated place to share their union. He choked on his tears and noticed that Molly's eyes were also full with tears: She felt the void in his heart and also missed dear daddy and Mike back in the woods of Appalachia, one gasping for air, and the other trying to move his paralyzed legs.

The rings were finally exchanged and words of devotion spoken, and there were on their knees exchanging vows of love and devotion in front of Jesus on a simple wooden cross chopped off from a forest tree by the Pilgrims, as the keepers of the legend knew for sure.

That night Jim and Molly, now a married couple had a dinner in Ben's Warf on Cape Cod pier, sharing a simple wooden table with two large, candles bright exuding flashes of light and warmth, listening to jukebox playing her favorite Patty Page songs, with the blinking beacons of the fishing boats reflecting on the waves below, adding yet another page of timeless story of people passed by they could feel, yet not hear.

Three days later Jim, Molly and Mother Sarah were back on the way down to Appalachia, driving along the coast's winding roads, stopping for bite at small country stands and markets, then spending the night in darkened and sleepy motels whose name one felt like being familiar, but long forgotten.

On Fools Day, April 1st, 1957 there were back in Cold Hollow and found out that the joke was on them for sure.

Jim's New York buddy private investigator Elmer Quincy had penned him a letter regarding him long lost mother Ingrid Bedenbacher, who apparently had just returned from a POW camp in Russia after spending six years scrapping for gold on the frozen banks of river Kolyma in Siberia. She was admitted in veteran's hospital in really bad health condition and expected to be under medical care for at least a year.

Meanwhile, Marshal Beam has brought his wife Mabel and four young children from down South in Alabama to the house on the edge of Cold Hollow, just to find a burning cross on the front yard next day and sign scribbled on from porch, "N...r get out".

Jim had trouble handling his fury when passed by Sheriff Ernie Hatchet's two-room office next to Lorry's diner.

"I am putting $500 reward for the head of the misfit who threatened my yard man Marshal Beam, and you spread the word around that I'll hunt them hillbillies down and make sure they go to the slammer," he placed two checks on police counter.

"The other check is for $2000 dollars as a donation to your office to use as you please, just make sure that my main man is left alone, and I am giving

Marshal my shotgun to defend his family if he needs to, do you read me Ernie?" Jim voice hushed down to an angry whisper as he tried to hold down his anger.

"All right, all right Catfish, Roger to that, I read you loud and clear, I'll tell my deputy Clarence Mims to pass by the house every hour on his route, and pull over any meathead who is loitering the area, you got my word on it," Sheriff Hatched smiled as Jim slammed the door and walked out of the room.

Few day later he was back on the mountain to check his coal mine, and was treated with a pleasant surprise: Marshal Beams has been working very hard, delivering 200 tons of prime quality anthracite for a spectacular $7000 dollars by employing a part time man to speed the loading of the truck.

Jim and Molly life together started slow and bumpy, as she tried to accustom herself to her dad's and brother's disabilities, slowly leaning how to help with their medicines and rehab programs, instead of crying when they would limp nearby.

In her new role of a healer and consoler, Molly soon regained self-confidence, continuing to absorb the ills and the blessings of that milky blind world she had lived for years, and eventually sparks of happiness and joy started flashing from her bright blue eyes. Then she got the best news in the world: The doctor confirmed that she was pregnant with twins, due in the summer of 1958.

"How will we name them," she would poke at Grandma Taylor and Jim.

"Two girls Taylor and Sarah, two boys Jim and George, and boy and a girl scramble of both," they would joke, leaving her even more perplexed.

Time went slowly in expectation of their big event, as many times Jim would put his ear on her tummy and try to listen to the movements inside, and get instead a mule like kick when the babies moved around.

"Them children sure kick like Frances folks, don't they," he would complain to Grandma Taylor.

"They will be copy of you and her, sweet little trouble makers you'll would hate to spank some times, but love to kiss always," she will return with another joke.

After months of fear, joys, cries and suspicions, the big day came with the biggest gift one can ever imagine: a little girl and boy they named Mary Taylor and George Gordon, two little cuties wrapped in white baby blankets sleeping in their mother's arms.

"It took a second and a bullet to kill the North Korean soldier back in Pusan, and probably twenty years for his mom and dad to raise him," Jim was thinking for himself, suspiciously looking around, fearing that someone may read his thoughts.

"That damn war and whoever made it were the most horrible thing one can imagine, and wish I could look his dad in the face and say "I am sorry"", a lump went through his throat and few tears slid down Jim's face.

But the clouds and sorrows of the past soon gave way to joy and happiness: Jim was now a father, a millionaire, a highly decorated US veteran whose country has recognized with its with highest medals, a respected and adored leader of his community, in other words recipient of the American dream and everything that it stood for.

Back in Korea life had thought James Francis Tom one sure lesson: We human are vulnerable beings. The sudden whims of the Providence could rip apart man's life in a second, and only prayers for Divine protection can lead us out the dark forest of evil deeds, and into the bright sunny meadows of Christian life in a search of peace and consolation. He had survived two impossible confrontations with misfortune and death, and had been blessed to live and tell about it. But deep inside his mind he could hear the whispers of Uncle George urging cautions and warnings Jim could not understand. He did not have to wait much longer to find what was he up against.

Chapter 4

The Cave In

It has been raining for almost a week in Cold Hollow when the last Friday of October 1957 came, Jimmy and his three workers laboring the whole day to send the last two loads of #7 coal to Consolidated Mines downhill. Marshal Beam had taken a leave to go down to Alabama, load all his personal property and haul it to house at the end of Cold Hollow.

Jim decided to spend the night in the office, then finish some small chores in the morning and drive down to mountain to spend the weekend with the family.

On the second day on the mine, the sky suddenly cleared and patches of blue became visible between clusters of clouds flying over the mountain. Jimmy walked around the base of the chapel, shovel in hand, scooping dead branches and other debris that have slid with the mudflow down the hill. A sudden flash of sunshine blinded him for a moment, and he looked up to the sky, just to see a reddish reflection of something among the trees up on the nearly vertical cliff. Flabbergasted by his vision, he trained his eyes in the direction of mysterious flash, but there was nothing unusual among the grass and dead frozen brush on the hill. Half an hour later he was all done clearing the debris and leaves around the chapel base, so he put the shovel on his shoulder and walked back to mine's office when a sudden burst of wind shook the trees and there was a sound of breaking branch. Jim looked up the hill, and there was again a brownish reflection of something among the brush on the sharp incline.

"May be a natural chunk of copper," he thought, then walked in the office and picked up Uncle George binoculars. The large field of view placed the brush and sages cover face of the bluff plain in his eyes, and there it was; a vertical irregular piece of brown/reddish metal squeezed between two enormous pieces of rock.

"Must be a placer deposit of copper on the property with the real vein deep within the mountain," Jim decided, walking back to the warmth of the office.

Jimmy loaded up a backpack with 100 feet of rope and climbing gear he found on Uncle George office closet, then took a narrow foot trail that seem to be winding up toward the hills top.

Some hours later, exhausted after climbing through the thick brush and young trees that have found roots on the side of the mountain, he found himself just above the two rocks that appeared to have the mysterious reddish chunk in between them. It took another half an hour to drop the rope downhill and slowly lower himself in. The final push of the side of the cliff sent him crashing down at the base of the rocks, and right in front of a curiously curved, nearly smooth slice of what appeared to eight feet copper slice squashed between the mountain's face. Jimmy ran his hand across the cold metal, pushed the surface sideways and suddenly felt a movement along the curve, then pushed again even harder on what he was already sure to be a copper cylinder. It kept rolling until revealed a narrow, square opening as warm air rushed in his face and make his heart miss a bit. Jimmy lit his miner's headlight and carefully shone a beam inside: it was a narrow passage cut in the mountain that appeared to curve to the right.

Even a decorated hero like Jimmy was hit by a sudden flash of fear as he realized that should he get trapped by something inside, his Pusan mortal fight with the North Korean submachine nest will look like walk in the park on 4th of July.

"I must block the cylinder from rolling back with a piece of rock, then get inside and investigate where the pathway is leading to," he was talking to himself, trying to slow down the fear that had fallen upon him.

After dragging a piece of triangular rock into the base of the slit, he stepped in, dragging a piece of rope through the darkness broken by the flickering flashes of his mining light.

Jimmy counted forty paces until he reached a large cavity that was open to what appeared to be a valley under bright, sunny sky with hundreds of yellow topped Indian tepees meandering along a white foam covered boonie river rushing down the mountain.

He stood in bewilderment for few minutes with his eyes scanning this bright but unknown world until he noticed that next to the sidewall of the cave there were three large pointed stones around a fireplace, and a carving that appeared to be a map. If the Ranger division of US army ever taught him something, it was the skill to read maps, and Jimmy never seen one like it, with Japan bulging quarter way in the Pacific, Philippines spreading over Australia, Russia and Alaska joined together, and old England spreading down to the Azores.

Sudden screams and laughter of flock of children threw him back to the world, little fingers pulling his shoe strings and shirt buttons, other trying to adjust his wrist watch. Then the commotion died down as ten warriors led by an older man in white attire with long white-combed hair below his knees and golden amulet on his chest froze in front of him.

Jimmy bowed his head on a sign of respect, and uttered a greeting in Lakota he had learned from Molly.

"I brought you fire," he respectfully whispered, then extended his hand forward, cigarette lighter in hand, and pressed the flint button. A kindle of fire shined in the near darkness of the cave, with children screaming in horror and the warriors pointing their fletchers at him.

The Chief with the golden amulet did not even blink an eye, just extended his open right arm to Jim, as wanting the magic object in the palm of his hand. The man carefully rubbed the shiny object in his hands, and then looked at him with eyes asking, "How do I do that?"

Jim again bowed his head in respect, his hand turned the lighter upward, guiding Chief's pointer finger to the flint button. A bright kindle of fire appeared again, there was another wave of children's screams, but now the shaman waved his left hand to quiet them down, screaming in Lakota "Pheta Oihankesni, Pheta Oihankesni."

It was not clear to Jim what the shaman has just said, but it was very plain that after his play with fire a good whiff of excitement has fallen over his children and warriors.

Chief clapped his hands three times, and then two young women brought a brown leather bag, placing it in his hands. Two large teardrop glass like objects were in Jim's hands, as Chief again clapped his hands three times, muttering the words "Wakhan thanka ista, Wakhan thanka ista, "and then pointing at his eyes.

Jim heart told him he has been given sacred objects of Lakota, perhaps "Eyes of God", bowed his head in respect, and then started backing off to the narrow pathway cut in the mountain.

It took four hours for him to climb down the slippery hill, facing sudden gusts of cold wind and waves of drizzle that was blinded his eyes, trying not to lose balance dragging all ropes and gear to finally end up back down in Uncle George's office. Jim carefully wrapped in linen cloth the two glass ovals gifted to him by the mysterious tribal shaman behind the copper door up the hill, then lit the big cast iron stove and stuffed it with shiny chunks of coal, took his mud soaked booths and stretched in front of the warm fire, carefully writing down in Uncle's George diary all the magic words spoken to him by the Lakota Chief.

A good sip of moonshine gave him warmth, and he descended in a bumpy sleep interrupted by faces and voices of people jumping at him in sudden flashes of light and then pale away, angry rain drops beating on shack's window and sound of pouring rain falling on the metal roof.

When Jim woke up on Saturday morning, the fire in the stove has died down a bit, but the rain above was still pounding the mountain. He rekindled the fire, cooked himself a quick breakfast, and then walked outside to be met by low, gray rain clouds covering fog submerged hilltops, sound of water running down the hill gulley's towards mine's entrance.

Jim was just about to lock up the gate and turn on the bilge pumps, and then turn around and leave when he heard mining cart #2 make a noise, like sliding a half wheel turn downhill.

"Damn rain is soaking up the mountain and rafters are settling down," he thought, attaching a large chain to the cart and then fishing the eye above the steel door beam.

"Now you ain't going nowhere, honey," he admonished the cart, turning again to the gate on the way out.

There was a loud rafter moaning followed by the sound of the cart sliding another turn down to the pit.

"C'mon now old lady, don't let me spend the night here," he said, then waited for the noise to come at him, but there was none.

"That's a girl, my girl, you be good now," he smiled at the mining cart, caressing the cold steel handle with his hand, and then headed for the gate.

A raw, low pitch growl came from the pit, noise of sliding heavy rafters, then like a river breaching a mountain high dam a stream of mud and coal spilled from the sides of the pit, lifting him upward and toward the exit.

Jimmy knew that a black death was to come upon him soon, and desperately tried to reach the chain of cart #2 hoisted to the eye above the entrance, blind fear pushing his arms up, away from the strangle of the grey, muddy river of coal below. Pulling himself up and walking on chunks of coal, he was trapped below the steel entry beam, head outside in the drizzling rain, sharp pain in his rib cage, no feeling at all below the waist, then the spill suddenly stopped, his eyes looking down on a mountain of muddy debris with sharp coal tips pocking the surface.

His pale world was running out flying over the battlefield in Pusan, field covered by scattered dead bodies of Korean soldiers, then suddenly he saw Molly Crains sitting on the riverbank, her blue eyes gliding over the waves, away from him.

Then there was long silence, long, long silence.

"I must dead, really dead, a survivor of the bloodiest battle of the Korean war, just to come home and get crushed in a coal mine cave in," thoughts were flying through his head, again sinking in an endless sea of white silence, a helpless flash of light, just a spirit wandering over the waves.

Chapter 5

Talking to Clouds

Benton Jennings and his son Curly had two really good days up on the mountain, cutting some nice cherry and oak hardwood stumps from his lot at Glory Pass, then spent the Friday night in grandpa's cabin of the ridge. Early Saturday morning Benny did not like the cold rain drizzling at his Chevy truck loaded with their lumber treasure, so he and Curly took the muddy road downhill to Cold Hollow, carefully trying to stay away from the mudflows that were already breaking from the brush covered hills. When they made it down to Twin Rainbow pass and were just about to turn away from Uncle's George chapel, headlight beam traversed along the mine entrance and a strange flash of red caught the sharp eye of Curly.

"Dad, there is man on the coal pile, pull over, let me check him out," he screamed, pointing towards mine's entrance.

Stopping a heavy-laden Chevy on a muddy road ain't easy at all, and Benny knew that from a bitter experience, so he pumped the brake pedal few times and managed to slide the truck on a small gravel shoulder on the side.

Curly led him toward the coal pile, with Benny trying to stay straight on his bowed legs sliding in the mud, until they made it to mine's entrance. Up there below to a sign reading "#Dig 17", right below the front steel girder there was a body of a man, head covered with bloody mud, hands buried in chunks of coal.

"Dear Lord, my army buddy "Jim Catfish Francis" is laying here, go get couple shovels from the office and let's dig him out," he hollered at Curly, pointing to the office shed on the side. It took a good half of an hour to pull Jimmy out on flat piece of lumber, and thanks Lord he was still alive, puffs of air coming out of his lips after Benny wiped out his face with a towel soaked in clean water. US army had taught Benny of being a medic helper, and just by looking Jimmy, he already knew what to do: carefully scratch the bottom of his feet with his finger and look if his legs would move.

"Lordy Dearest, his back is broken," he whispered almost in tears, scanning around for something to lift up Jim and carry him to the office.

Like reading his thoughts, Curly already knew

that things were about to get even worst.

"Dad, the mudslide buried the office, the front doors are blocked by rocks," he moaned, then pointing towards the chapel, "Look, there is a casket on the front porch."

"Go get it and drag it up the pile," Benny ordered, then took his raincoat off and covered Jim with it.

Curly came back dragging a crudely made, moist but relatively clean casket next to Jim, then helped Benny slide him on it and started dragging it back down towards the chapel, avoiding big chunks of coal that may split it to pieces.

The rain was furiously beating the front of the chapel, so Benny decided to kick the old door and push the casket inside. A smell of rotten wood and dead critters stunned their senses, making Curly exclaim," I'll bring a piece of rope to tie the lid around and a blanket to cover him up, this place stinks like snake pit. Let's drive down the hill and get Sheriff Hatchet to come with a medic and haul Jimmy to the hospital."

A half an hour later they were in police office, a patrolman and a medic warming the truck, Sheriff radioed he's on the way to Rainbow Ridge Pass with the patrol car and another 1st aid medical kit in it.

When the medic's truck finally made up the mine and officer Paisley pushed the door open, they could not believe the horror they were up against: A whole moving ring of critters, black moccasins and rattlers had woven around the gasket, hisses and flashing eyes in the darkness, coiling up ready to strike, keeping everyone away in fear.

Officer Paisley knew that unless they pulled Jim out of the casket and soon, he will die from a loss of blood, so he picked the radio and called on his boss:

"Sheriff Hatchet Sir, patrolman Paisley here, Jim's in a casket rounded up by damn moccasins and rattlers, could you pick-up Molly Crains and drag her here to chase them critters away?"

There were few minutes of static noise on the radio, then the crackling voice of Sheriff Hatchet came loud and clear over the radio:

"Rodger to that, I'll radio the National Guard and request an air ambulance to land down on the flat of the road, we'll be there shortly, 10-4," squelch click and radio was silent again.

A half an hour later Molly Crains and Sheriff Hatchet were in front of Jim's casket engulfed by rolling, coiling and hissing snakes.

Molly went silent, here lips whispering sacred words in Lakota, both hands with fingers spread around and pushing towards the critters, with Sheriff Hatchet and patrolman Paisley holding guns in hands, ready to shoot if a snake jumped at her.

But her magic was working, and slowly the critters started sliding away in the darkness until an enormous black moccasin stayed coiled on the top of the casket, ready to strike.

"I know how to take care of that, Molly please step aside," he carefully tried to pull Molly to the entrance but she exploded in rage, screaming at the snake, "Get away from my husband, get away or I will crush you in two," making a crushing gesture with her hands, then shouting something in Lakota.

But it was too late, the moccasin charged forward, there were three loud shots from police guns, and blood and snake parts flying covered the floor. Jim's casket was dragged on chapel's porch and lid open: Jim was still alive and the medic started connecting him to an oxygen bottle and bandaging his wounds.

An hour later he was on an air ambulance with Molly Crains next to him, flying over the mountains over to Charleston hospital where a team of surgeons were already awaiting him, courtesy of Governor Stevens phone call who had taken personal duty to save the life of one of his state most celebrated citizens. Incredible as it may seem, but Jim Francis Tom had survived yet another brush with death and won this time again but without a medal, yet unknown to him he was blessed by the Providence to see and experience miracles destined for him by the unknown ways of the Lord.

Chapter 6

Miracle of Twin Rainbow Ridge

Many months had passed since the mine cave in, an after four surgeries, hundreds of hours of rehab and plenty of rest, James Tom Francis was out of the hospital in a wheel chair pushed by Molly Crains, surrounded by well-wishers.

"You were blessed to survive against impossible odds, but coal mound near the mine entrance crushed two vertebrae and you'll never be able to walk more than few feet without help," surgeon Dr. Watson Kendrick warmly shook his hand on the way out. Flown back to Cold Hollow with an air ambulance again gave Jim time to look at the mountains below, already covered with fresh green branches the early spring has brought to life after the long, hard winter.

Back in Cold Hollow few surprises were awaiting him, with Marshal Beam and his family waiting at the flat next to road to meet them.

Three helpers were hired to push ten tons of coal per day down to the terminal, and bank account has grown by $26,000 dollars after Marshal has meticulously kept account of expenses and payments. All broken rafters have been replaced, coal carts railing replaced and half crushed Uncle George's office completely rebuild.

Jim was horrified by the magnitude of land slide when driven back to the mine: The whole hill above had slid down within feet from the chapel, surrounding it like giant palm of hand of brutal and surreal monster punctured by rocks, crushed trees and brushes.

Marshal had taken the liberty to call a cement man to dig a pad for the chapel, and then had someone with a tractor to put in on rollers and slide it on top of the cement pad.

"I am glad I met you on that sad, snowy day down on the train station, you are one good man," Jim shook the enormous hand of Marshal Beam.

"I am giving you a $2000 bonus for your hard work and good and honest heart."

Marshal was deeply touched by his generosity.

"Thank you much Mister James Francis Sir, I really do appreciate you gave chance to a branded man," his eyes were moist with tears, smile chocked by emotions.

There was a plan forming in Jim's brain, a vision of his chapel with all new seats and colored glass windows, and a large color mosaic depiction of the Savior with eyes made of the ovals gifted to him by the people behind the copper door up on the hill.

"I will call the Rowan Brothers to rebuild the chapel starting tomorrow, and I like you keep an eye on them hillbillies when I am not around," he shook Marshals hand before was driven back home.

Still too weak to drive and work in mine's office daily, Jim took another month and a half to regain strength and think straight about his new life as a disabled person.

Marshal came finally with the good news that his chapel has been all refinished and ready for him on a bright, humid day when they took up the windy road to the Twin Rainbow Ridge. When his chair rolled in the chapel and sweet smell of fresh pine graced his senses, Jim's eyes scanned the Savior's face and suddenly he was choked by tears: The ovals gifted to him by Lacota shaman up the hill behind the copper were Lords eyes now, and they were alive by flashes of sunlight and fast moving clouds above.

"He's talking to me, he's has been waiting for me all this time," his trembling hand pointed up to the Savior to Marshal's complete astonishment.

"Yes Sir Mr. Francis, The Lord has surely been waiting for you," Marshal smiled, tap him on the shoulder and walk out to the mine.

It took Jim about a half an hour to bring his heart beat down to quiet, then took a deep breath of air and whispered a question to the Lord, a question that has been on his mind for years:

"Shines, why should a man from Cold Hollow, West Virginia travel 5000 miles to Korea, just to toss six hand grenades at a machine gun nest, then shoot a young man in the eye and kill him? Why did you make us do that?" his voice was trembling, brilliant brown eyes staring in Lord's face.

Light clouds and streaks of sunshine were running like a lazy river and floating away, like if his voice was not heard.

"You don't want to say Shines?" his voice was low, crackling and disappointed, eye full with tears.

"Then someone else must be blamed for it, is the Devil who did it, Shines, did he bribed the politicians," Jim's eyes were again scanning Man's face for a hint or snub.

But this time Lord's eyes suddenly were covered with black clouds, streaks of lighting flashing in the distance, the sky suddenly cleared and then scattered light clouds were again floating over the mountain.

Jim knew that he had finally gotten an answer, screaming with last of his voice, "Thank you for speaking to me Lord, I surely appreciate it," then rolled the wheel chair back towards the door and went outside.

Flashes of sunshine met him as he low clouds were scraping the mountain tops with patches of fog and drizzle, then Jim suddenly realized something that has escaped hi attention at all.

"I could have been killed in the coal mine and never would have bothered to see my own mother," thought of guilt were crossing his mind, as he pushed himself down the ramp and strolled across the parking lot.

Back in the office, he took a company stationary

and wrote a letter to his army buddy, now a proud owner of a private detective agency in New York.

"Dear Elmer, I just got out of the hospital after a deadly cave in and realized that I could have been killed and never seen my mother Ingrid Bedenbacher, who as you know is currently residing in West Germany. I wonder if you may be interested to act on my behalf and get in touch with her, asking her to come and visits us here in West Virginia. If for some reason she is uncomfortable coming back to the US, try to arrange for us to meets her in London at time convenient for both of us. Please advise on retainers and fees involved. Yours Truly: Jim Francis."

He could not wait to go back to Cold Hollow and tell Gordon Crains that he may go back to Mother England after nearly two hundred years and visit Chester, the ancestral town of his folks. But knock on the door brought the news from the world to him a Marshal Beam walked in with magazine in his enormous hand.

"You is going to the moveis, ain't you boss?" he had a big smile on his face, spreading the "Coal Times" magazine on the desk.

Jim's eyes rolled over the text and photos in front of him, then he chuckled a noise of surprise and amazement after reading main article heading: "Governor Howard Ellison to name Cold Hollow resident James Francis Tom West Virginia's coal miner of the year."

"I recon I may be going to Charleston for have a victory lapse with my wheel chair, thank you Marshal," he warmly shook his hand.

"Listen, I am expecting an important letter from a friend of mine Elmer Quincy, be on the lookout for it when you pick up the mail, would you?" Jim waived his main man out, then pulled a stack of coal terminal receipts and the ledger book to finish his delivery audit.

The summer days were humid, busy and seemingly endless, as every morning Jim will spend hours in the office or inspect truck shipments on the way to the terminal, then will roll his wheel chair towards the chapel to have his lunch on the front porch, then spend a half an hour talking to the Man with eyes of a restless ocean. His mind will many times roll over the new life of Moly Crains as a now seeing person, and bouts of depression drowned in a jar of moonshine. Their twins

Cricket and Josh were five years old already, bright, curious, talking wise and smiling generously at any occasion, two blondies with hearts of gold that were counting the days to meet their long-lost grandma Ingrid.

The letter from Elmer Quincy finally arrived in October 1960, and the news was not particularly good.

"Dear Jim, we got in touch with your mom using the services of a detective agency in Stuttgart, and I need to report to you that she is receiving a medical care due to injuries she suffered as a POW in Russian gulag in Siberia. She is very excited to hear from you and is willing to travel to West Virginia with an assigned caretaker since she has trouble keeping balance and tires easily. The doctors are telling us that she will be cleared to travel by the next Spring, and that she would love to see photos of you and your children. Please use the post-stamped envelope to send her a letter and share with her all mementoes of your distinguished life, and don't forget your battle ribbons and medals from Korea. Yours sincerely, Elmer."

Jim treaded through the letter with his trembling fingers many, many times, trying to keep his heartbeat from rushing madly in his chest, wiping out tears rolling down his face from time to time.

"This is yet another threshold I must survive and get alive again," his thoughts were stricken by fear of the unknown, fear of crossing that endless divide in time that has taken his mom away from him for all those years.

During his lunch break, he spent long minutes in his chapel staring in the eyes of the Man with eyes of clouds over endless ocean, then mumbled a question that had been on his mind forever:

"Shines, why bless someone with cherished life, just to punished it by taking their loved ones away, why the torture and the brutally? Was it you who did the punishment?" Jim's voice was trembling in fear, moist fingers tapping on the handles of the wheelchair.

Light, puffy and gay clouds were rushing through the magic oval eyes of the Lord, flashes of sunlight breaking from above, blinding Jim for moment, before he risked asking the question that was on his thong.

"Shines, was it Evil who did the torture? Why didn't you stop him?"

A sudden growl of lightning striking the mountain shook the ground, violent sheet of shower drops beat the windows as if millions of fingers were knocking in anger, black grey menacing clouds slowly floated to the distance.

And then there was silence, sunlight sneaking in between the mountaintops.

"Shines, will I be forgiven and blessed to meet my mother?" Jim slid down on his knees, hands down on the floor, eyes up meeting eyes of the Lord, begging for forgiveness.

A warm, soft, living like gold glitter shone from above, and he knew the answer, pushing himself up in the wheelchair and strolling out in the bright world outside the chapel door.

Many months after this spiritual encounter, as Jim family and friends have gathered around the Christmas tree, he noticed that "Grandma Ingrid" picture has been framed by children and hanged up on the tree next to a small shiny airplane. Almost instantaneously, Jim had a premonition: "I must build a small plane airstrip opposite to "Twin Rainbow Ridge" so when Mom comes to visit West Virginia, she can land right next to mine's office, instead clunking around the dirt roads below."

The thought gave him so much strength that week after the holydays that he purchased the flat acre lot across the chapel and had someone with a dozer hauling out dead brush and sharp stones. But his vision had a millennia's old and unforgiving enemy: the brutal West Virginia winter. Soon ice cold drizzle turned into endless wave of snow that was blown around by vicious gusts of wind that soon forced closing of Twin Rainbow Ridge pass, and shut the mine for a week until dozer made it safe to climb up the mountain.

Trapped below in the valley in front of a welcome and warm fireplace with Molly and the kids for a week, Jim got a long-awaited letter from Mother Ingrid with few hands drawn water color paintings between the pages. One old and yellowish aged picture caught his eyes at once: Young woman with a baby signed, "New York, 1936", the same image Jim had found in Uncle George's drawer desk in the mine's office.

The letter finally brought the story that had been denied to him for 35 years:

"Dear Son, I will never forgive myself for leaving

you with your father George in 1936, but as an employee of German company that was a front for German Military Intelligence the Abwehr, I was ordered to return home or face possible espionage charges as the drums of war became louder by the day. My position as a radio operator was a top-secret assignment, and had I been arrested by Hoover's FBI, the lives of you and your completely oblivious father George would have been ruined forever. Going home did not change my life for the better because I got captured by the Red Army and sent to special camp in Siberia where we all were treated harshly and without any mercy. I am scheduled to have two surgeries to help restore my ability to walk freely, but otherwise I am well for a 65-year-old woman, and counting every second of the day to come and embrace you and your wonderful family back in America. Love, Mother Ingrid."

Jim held the pages in his hand for a long time, looking outside as the snow kept pilling in and darkness fell over the valley.

"Is Grandma Ingrid coming soon Daddy?" Cricket and Josh startled him, as his mind and soul had gone so far out, that coming back to nearly a minute or so, as he was staring at his children.

"Maybe she'll be coming early spring, let's pray for that, come and give daddy a hug, would you sweethearts?" He held them warm and close, trying to suppress his tears before sending them back to their beds.

In a month or so the roads softened up and work in the mine resumed at full speed, and so did the dozer man who finally was able to grade a 1500 feet landing strip and install landing lights and a small wing tee tower. Jim was even able to get an aviation frequency radio set installed in the mine's office, and a second one back in his house, and with this there was only one thing to do: Wait for Mother Ingrid to arrive from Germany.

The cold and snowy winter did not go away easily, as it was trying to torture Jim and test his fortitude before granting his most cherished wish to welcome his long lost mother to the family embrace.

Time kept trickling slow and lazy, as every day of the week except Sunday Jim will be driven to the mine's office, work until noon, then have his lunch in chapel foyer. He would then roll his wheelchair inside and stare for long time in the eyes of the Savior, expecting as if a single word or a flash of his eye to bridge the burden of time and unveil welcome news.

Spring finally arrived, sprinkling trees with greens and blossoms on the hills, as patches of blue skies became brighter by day, and sudden storms would thunder in the distant mountains, painting pale rainbows on the horizon.

On a warm, sunny April day Jim had snoozed up in his wheelchair right after lunch in the chapel when loud voices of children running in startled him immensely:

"Daddy, Daddy get up, Grandma Ingrid just landed across the road, let's go meet her," Cricked and Josh were pulling his hands, eyes shining in excitement, voice chirping like little birds.

Half asleep, Jim had trouble comprehending the words, his eyes running around their faces like looking for a joke or prank, but there was none. Then suddenly he bolted out of his wheelchair seat and ran after them out on the parking lot towards the landing strip. He could see the freshly mowed grass and the red Studebaker surrounded by Molly Crains, Grandma Taylor and Marshal Beam talking to a white haired old lady, right next to the small step ladder leading to the cockpit.

Cricket and Josh reached Mother Ingrid first and she hug them close to her, and then Jim slid on the wet grass with his welcoming arms extended forward towards her, crying, "Mother, is that you, after all those years?"

She looked at him with her brilliant brown eyes, wiping tears falling down her cheeks.

"Yes it is me, finally me my dearest son whom I abandoned as a baby," her voice was dry a crackling from emotion.

Jim jumped on his feet and grabbed Mother Ingrid and embraced her, then noticed something very strange: Marshal Beam's eyes were wide open and confused, his big hands wiping his face.

"What are you all crying about, smile, my Mom is with us, please smile."

Marshal pointed to his legs.

"You ran two hundred yards from the chapel in few minutes boss, two hundred yards after I've been pushing your wheelchair for years."

Jim felt like smacked by a soft hammer on the head as he looked down the wet grass, his pants all wet and green from sliding down.

"I recon I did run two hundred yards after all, didn't I," he mumbled confusedly, then ran to Molly Crains and screamed with all his voice: "You ain't no blind sugar, and I no crippled no more, we got a miracle, Mother Ingrid gifted us a miracle."

Marshal Beam pointed away to the misty horizon.

"Look Ms. Ingrid, look out at twin rainbows over the Blue Ridge mountains, that's why people has called those ridges."

And they all embraced, hand over each other's shoulder, staring at the pulsing dance of red, green and blue lights towering over rain clouds covered distant peaks with lush forest carpet below, a blind woman blessed with sight, a crippled man gifted with a walk, and two former prisoners born free again.

James Francis Tom had a strange tingle on back of his head, as if someone little fingers were tickling his neck, asking him to look back. And sure enough, his searching eyes saw right on the top of the hill where the magic people behind the copper door have lived in peace for eternity, the Lacota white haired Shaman with his golden amulet shining in the Sun, his children and warriors behind him in arrow formation over the hill.

He raised his hand and waived and them, and the Holy man and the children waived back.

"They knew the future, they surely knew all along," a stray thought went through his head, then he turned his eyes forward just to meet his mother's shining

brown eyes.

"They knew everything, didn't they?" she whispered.

"I saw them in Russia over the snow-covered hills of Siberia,"

"They are immortal."